How to Play
Air Guitar

How to Play

Air Guitar

All the Greatest Moves from your Guitar Heroes

Ian West & Steve Gladdis

Chrysalis
Impact

First published in 2002 by Chrysalis Impact.
An imprint of Chrysalis Books plc
64, Brewery Road.
London N7 9NT
United Kingdom

A member of **Chrysalis** Books plc
© 2002 Chrysalis Books plc

ISBN 1 84411 003 6

Text © Ian West and Steve Gladdis 2002
Volume © Chrysalis Books plc 2002

Distributed in the United States and Canada by Sterling Publishing Co.,
387 Park Avenue South, New York, NY 10016, USA

Credits
Project management: Laura Ward
Photography: Neil Sutherland
Model: Matt Russell
Designed by Grade Design Consultants, London

Printed and bound in China
Corbis UK Ltd for photographs on pages 10 and 11

Acknowledgements
The authors wish to thank Al King, whose unique skills have been invaluable in the
development of this guide. Thanks also to Matt Russell for being a true genius and
a good sport. Thanks to the Great Frog, Carnaby Street, London, for lending the
silver Snake Dreams' ring for the photograph on page 13. Last but certainly not
least, heartfelt thanks to Kate Kirby for nurturing this book.

Contents

Foreword

I first became World Champion in August 2001. I'd travelled with the 13 members of the British team (seven competitors, six roadies) to the city of Oulu in Finland, the "mecca" of air guitar some 80 miles south of the Arctic Circle. I'd never played air guitar before and considered my "cold" entry into the championship as an ordeal to test a man's verve and panache. I was extremely nervous.

On that fateful evening, I watched contestant after contestant perform the classics of rock in front of 3,000 black-metal rock enthusiasts and the world's press, and I figured that I'd never be able to create a persona the way they did on stage. My knees were shaking and my heart was beating like a badly tuned engine. I feared that I was unworthy of the contest, and I feared ridicule.

Instead, in the heat of the floodlights, I found something which gave me the courage to sacrifice myself at the altar of rock.

And that's how it is with air guitar. Like love, it is a pure abstract, within the grasp of everyone. It is unbreakable and it will purify your very soul.

If you're holding this book then I guess you, too, are part of this same disparate family. Like so many illegitimate children spawned throughout this fertile land by the kings of rock, we are connected by a thin trail of seed that has left subtle yet definite similarities in our make-up – and I have been brought in to stick the pages of this book together with the insight of global recognition.

So I tell you this: air guitar is an inviolable art form and it is also the last tool we possess to reclaim the virtual world with our own hands. Look after it.

Zac Monro, World Air Guitar Champion 2001

Introduction

Congratulations! You've just taken your first step towards learning how to play air guitar. Once you've mastered this challenging instrument, all the thrill of playing live to a packed stadium can be yours. Suitable for all standards of air guitarist, this book will take the absolute beginner from novice to hero. Even the most seasoned pro will find plenty of new avenues to explore. Age should not impede you – it's never too early or too late to start strumming. All you need is a little guidance, a willingness to learn and a complete and utter lack of self-dignity.

Since homo erectus first made music, the human race has divided naturally into two distinct groups: the musically gifted and the musically challenged. Many of us mortals have sought stardom, but have been cruelly held back by a total inability to sing or to play a note. This book is dedicated to those individuals who have all the energy and passion it takes to deliver a world-class performance, but who fall at the first hurdle due . . . to a lack of basic talent.

To smooth your progression from bedroom star to rock god, the book is divided into expertly choreographed "lessons". Each one encapsulates a range of classic stances, crowd-pleasing moves and facial expressions appropriate to that level. Included with the book is a free inflatable guitar for you to practise your art.

In sum, all the tips and techniques required to turn you into an air guitar virtuoso are contained in these pages. Amaze your friends, impress the opposite sex and thrill imaginary crowds of thousands. Read on and prepare to rock.

Note: All the exercises in this book are configured for the right-handed air guitarist. If you are left-handed, please reverse all moves. Your air guitar should not need re-stringing.

1 The History of Air Guitar

Air guitar first came into the musical mainstream in the middle of the twentieth century, with the invention of the electric guitar and the birth of rock 'n' roll. However, since time immemorial, the human desire to show off has spurred individuals to accompany the music of their age, whatever form it happened to take.

Thus the modern air guitarist is actually the musical descendant of a long line of artists stretching back through history to the dawn of civilisation. Here is just a handful of early examples of those who have obeyed our most primitive instinct to gyrate, strut and generally make an exhibition of ourselves – also referred to as prancing about like a fool.

Cave paintings unearthed in Southern France show clearly that the history of air guitar began several thousand years earlier than scientists had previously assumed. In the prehistoric wall painting (right). the figure at the top is thought to be performing in a ceremony to give thanks for a successful hunt.

This Egyptian example shows Ramesses III relaxing in his court while one of his concubines plays an air lyre. Hieroglyphs reveal that Nubian slaves trained in the art were highly prized: 20 were interred in the Great Pyramid with the mummified Ramesses to perform for him in the afterlife.

During festivals in Ancient Greece followers of Bacchus, god of wine and merriment, would perform in his honour on the air lyre.

This magnificent statue from Ephesus shows a maiden in mid-strum. (Note the fashion at the time of performing topless. which was hugely popular with the spectators.)

9

CHAPTER 1

Lesser-known Exponents

GEORGE W. BUSH ROCKS A YOUTH FORUM
IN THE RACE FOR THE PRESIDENCY.

JOHN PAUL SHOWS
YOU ARE NEVER TOO
OLD TO GET DOWN.

PRINCE CHARLES HAS ADMITTED TO
FLIRTING WITH THE AIR GUITAR
IN HIS YOUTH. HIS PERFORMANCES
REGULARLY HAD HIS UNIVERSITY
CHUMS IN STITCHES. NOTE
ORIGINAL USE OF THE STRAW HAT.

2 Before you Begin

If you follow the exercises in this book, it shouldn't be too long before you feel totally at home with the air guitar – with the right guidance, you really can just "pick up and play". However, before you leap headlong into this exciting new world, it's important to make some simple preparations in order to facilitate the learning process and avoid some basic pitfalls.

First – and before you even pick up your air guitar – it's essential to get the right look. Remember, truly great performances start with truly huge attitude. If you look the part, you'll feel more confident and will already be on your way to becoming a bedroom rock god.

Follow these simple steps to adopt the right crowd-pleasing, groupie-thrilling air guitar image.*

* Bear in mind that some air guitar moves are highly strenuous. During early practice sessions, you may want to wear loose-fitting clothes that won't restrict your moves. Remember, when Jimi Hendrix first experimented with setting fire to his guitar, he wasn't on stage wearing a satin shirt and velvet loons with 28-inch bellbottoms – no, he was probably in a shed at the bottom of his garden in an old T-shirt and some faded sweat pants he didn't mind combusting.

The ideal T-shirt should allow freedom of movement. It should show off armpit hair (vital) and any chest hair (good, but not essential). Don't worry about any mysterious stains – these will just add to the air of a hard livin', hard drinkin', messy eatin' maverick.

Suitable examples include the well-loved ol' number with a faded logo of your band of choice.

The leather jacket – instant James Dean credibility.

On the bottom half, anything goes. The classic look would be jeans or leather trousers, with spandex for the truly adventurous. NOTE! With denim, spandex or leather, trousers should be worn so tight the audience can tell your religion.

Another good look is the skanky looking vest. This works particularly well when stretched tight over an ever-growing belly.

Footwear – the true maestro would go for a pair of snakeskin cowboy boots with a decent Cuban heel. If your budget won't stretch to these, you can make do with any trainers that look as though they have seen a bit of life.

Other good additions include chunky silver jewellery.

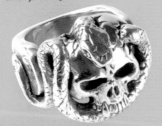

Ones to avoid: you are not going to look the part by wearing a Britney Spears T-shirt. Also, avoid any boy bands or animal charity logos – remember, you are trying to look mad, bad and dangerous to know.

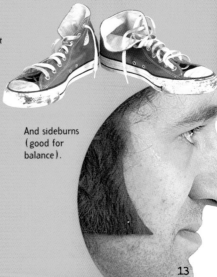

And sideburns (good for balance).

stretching

It is vital to warm up properly. The last thing you need is to be explaining at the Accident and Emergency department of the hospital that you pulled a groin muscle while performing a high kick during the middle section of "Bohemian Rhapsody".

"You'd better

those ch

Stretch the arms . . .   . . . and the waist . . .   . . . and the legs . . .   . . . and, finally, relax.

To prepare your face for the full range of expressions, stretch every muscle (the lips may need coaxing out of their beer-drinking position).

Use of Props

As a beginner, you may find it useful to play the inflatable guitar until you have mastered your moves and are ready to move on to the real thing – your air guitar. This will help you to position your hands properly and to master basic strumming. Blow up your guitar and prepare to dazzle.

If you puncture your inflatable guitar accidentally (say, due to a carelessly placed cigarette or by playing too clo[se] to spiky houseplants) DO NOT DESPA[IR]

You can continue your practice using many common household objects. You could try "The Spade".

Or improvise with anything else that comes to hand.

"The Duster"

"The Mop"

"The Spade"

"A tennis racquet can help the beginner with essential hand-eye co-ordination"

Use of Beer (a.k.a. "Music Oil"

You'll almost certainly have noticed that a whole range of everyday skills can be dramatically improved with increased beer consumption – for example, dancing, playing pool, telling jokes and the like.

These rules apply to the air guitar, too!

Readily available up and down the country, in bottled or canned form, beer is the secret weapon of the novice air guitarist. Application of beer loosens up your limbs, reduces your dignity levels and helps you truly to express yourself during intense solos.

A WORD OF CAUTION! THE GENERAL RULE IS AS FOLLOWS: THE MORE BEER YOU DRINK, THE BETTER YOUR PERFORMANCE. HOWEVER, THIS ONLY WORKS UP TO A CERTAIN POINT. OVERDO THE OL' MUSIC OIL AND YOU WILL LOSE CO-ORDINATION, LEADING TO SLOPPY STRUMMING, DRIBBLING AND FALLING OVER. VOMIT IS ALSO LIKELY TO SEND YOUR AIR GUITAR STRINGS OUT OF TUNE. THE FOLLOWING PICTORIAL GUIDE WILL HELP YOU TO JUDGE YOUR OWN OPTIMUM LUBRICATION LEVEL.

"Too stiff, more beer required"

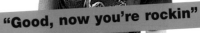

"Good, now you're rockin"

"...u may have overdone it"

"Too much has been imbibed, go to bed and try again tomorrow"

Getting Started

Well done! You're now ready for your first steps along the road to world rock superstardom. Don't be nervous – remember, Rome wasn't built in a day. At first, you may struggle with your unfamiliar instrument. If you do, imagine a young Eddie Van Halen, brow furrowed in concentration as his fingers fumble with his first atonal chord, or maybe even a teenage Brian May overdoing the "music oil" and passing out altogether. Even the greatest musicians had to start somewhere. Any mistakes you make in these early stages will have been made by countless others before you.

To avoid looking too much like a novice, you would be well advised to steer clear of these common mistakes:

Too Stiff
Don't just stand there like a scarecrow - think fluid, think sexy, think Freddie Mercury.

Staring at your Shoes
You are not trying out for an indie band. Don't stare at your shoes - look up and please that audience.

ego

attitude

confidence

REMEMBER! The three keys to great performance are **Ego**, **Attitude** and **Confidence**. Blow up that guitar, put on some ass-kicking tunes and let's get that mojo working!

Looking at your Hands
When you are playing, let the music take over. Give in to the beat, let the rhythm fill you and don't get too hung up on what your hands are doing – with time, your co-ordination will improve.

Tuning Up

If your instrument hasn't been played for some time, it may be out of tune. Screw up your face and assume a look of concentration. Cock your head to one side. Twang cautiously with your right hand, while twiddling intently with the air-tuning keys (at the pointy end). Peer down at your left hand with an air of total absorption, glancing occasionally down at the right hand. Nod with satisfaction after a few minutes.

(Don't waste too much time on this stage. When you are a huge star, you will probably have a roadie to take care of all this before you even get on stage.)

"Squint at your left hand in an expert fashion"

Strumming

The right hand is the driving force of your air guitar performance. Experiment by varying the length of your strum – long sweeps for crashing chords and a shorter, choppy action for the jangly bits.

Aim to keep your wrist loose and to get a good follow-through. Finally, don't worry if you are not blessed with a natural sense of rhythm – your strumming will improve as your confidence grows.

Figure 1   Figure 2

Left Hand

The key point to remember is that no truly great tune was ever composed using only one note (except perhaps "The Ace of Spades" by Motorhead). To maintain credibility, you will have to play up and down the fretboard. Don't bust a gut trying to match the music note-for-note, but keep that left hand moving!

The purist wouldn't hold anything in the right hand other than an air plectrum. However, you can use a real plectrum if you prefer, or substitute this with a coin or washer.

The strap length will determine the height of the strum - if you are unsure, begin at crotch level (Fig. 1). Use bold right-hand strokes, up and down in time to your chosen music.

The height of the strum also depends on the style of music you are playing. For jazz-funk, keep the air strap short (Fig. 2), so that the air guitar rests a few inches below your chin. For hard rock, keep the strap long and the air guitar slung low (Fig. 3). The beginner should play in the way he or she feels comfortable.

Some useful chord shapes

Figure 3

4 Beginners

Now the fun part begins. You have got yourself the right look and stretched your limbs out thoroughly. You have lubricated your tonsils and tuned up your guitar. You are now ready to take your instrument in your trembling hands and to start making some noise! Feel the spirit of the great performers throughout the ages fill you as we start the first lesson.

RECOMMENDED TUNE:
"BREAKIN' THE LAW" –
JUDAS PRIEST

Standard Legs Spread
Plant your feet firmly. Keep your centre of gravity low for maximum stability and push your crotch forward. This is your standard "Air Guitar Stance", suitable for most tunes.

Be wary of over-extending your spread. If you experience any groinal discomfort, bring your feet closer together. Or consult a specialist.

Foot up on Monitor
For intricate solos and tricky bits, you will need to get one foot up on the monitor. (A beer crate or your bed will make an adequate substitute.)

The Boogie

From the basic legs-spread stance, shift your weight from one leg to the other. Get a steady rhythm going, and sway from one side to the other like a polar bear in the zoo. The greatest exponents of this move are the gentlemen of Status Quo, who have built a career spanning four decades around this move and three chords.

When you have got your sway going, you can walk upstage and towards the audience using a scissoring walk – one foot being placed dead in front of the other.

"The rocking movement will soon have you in a deep trance"

The Standard Jump

A guaranteed crowd-pleaser, this is best done with a flourishing strum and a "look-at-me!" eyes-wide expression.
Bend your legs to get some height. Now spring up and tuck both feet in towards your butt.

RECOMMENDED TUNE:
"SONG 2" – BLUR

Bend your knees, and get ready for the take-off – remember, you're aiming to get as much height as possible.

"Cool, calm and collected"

If you haven't got a speaker stack. you could practise this move by jumping from your bed or your desk at work.

"One to make the fans go wild"

The Windmill

This is basically a 360-degree sweep with the right, strumming hand. Ideal for crashing chords, grand finales or whipping up the crowd for your opening number. The Who's Pete Townsend made this move famous. However, you should exercise caution. Once, Pete impaled his hand on the whammy bar of his guitar while executing the windmill, and had to be rushed to hospital. Although this problem shouldn't affect the air guitarist, it is inadvisable to attempt the windmill in rooms with low ceilings or crystal chandeliers.

RECOMMENDED TUNE: "WON'T GET FOOLED AGAIN" - THE WHO

"Squint those eyes, look really mean"

Note glazed, fixed expression. Bring down strumming hand aggressively over strings. Show that guitar who's daddy.

"Really show that guitar who's boss"

33

Faces

The finishing touch to your performance. The appropriate use of facial expressions will mark you out as a true virtuoso – such contortions help to demonstrate that you are connecting with your instrument and really feeling the music. Here are a few classics to get you started.

RECOMMENDED TUNE:
"GET IT ON" – T REX

"The Nonchalant"

So cool it hurts – despite your brilliance, your facial expression gives away none of your skill and craftsmanship. Your audience is enthralled; you are unconcerned. You could be waiting for a bus, not playing to thousands of adoring fans.

"The Pout"

RECOMMENDED TUNE:
"ANARCHY IN THE UK"
– THE SEX PISTOLS

"The Overbite"

Showing plenty of teeth."The Overbite" is a
good. all-round standby expression.

RECOMMENDED TUNE:
"PARANOID"
– BLACK SABBATH

5 Intermediate

Now you're cooking! If you have mastered the previous lesson, you'll be feeling pretty confident and ready to take on new challenges. If you want to try something a little more ambitious, read on and prepare to move up to the next level.

REMEMBER! Don't try to run before you can duckwalk – never forget the importance of warming up and applying the right level of liquid inspiration. Use what you have already learned and then weave a few of these more complex stances, moves and expressions into your routine. Keep it lively, and keep pushing your audience – you want them hanging on your every move. So turn that stereo up to eleven, and let's go!

Sharing the Mic

Of course, you won't always be playing alone. For a classic interaction with real or imagined band members, stand back to back and about a metre apart, and then lean in so that your backs meet – now both sing into the same mic.

One Hand in the Air

This is the ideal pose for when you have left a monstrous note hanging in the air, and are saluting the audience. It's also perfect for when you're singing along to a great rock anthem, such as the opening bars of Queen's "We Will Rock You". (Feel free to punch the air.)

RECOMMENDED TUNE:
"BROWN SUGAR"
– THE ROLLING STONES

37

The Pointing Windmill

This starts off like the basic windmill (see previous chapter) and is also suitable for power chords, but it has one important and tricky final flourish.

   The right hand makes a majestic sweep anti-clockwise (check direction in mirror) and crashes across the crotch. But, on the follow-through, the hand ends up pointing into the audience as if to say, "I am a rock god, you are a nubile groupie – see you back at the hotel." (Best used with a full pout.)

RECOMMENDED TUNE:
"YOU REALLY GOT ME"
– THE KINKS – FINALE

"I wanna hear

you scream"

**Some useful
pointing shapes**

**"See you back
at the hotel"**

The Scissor Jump

This is where you'll appreciate the importance of warming up. Bend your knees and spring up as though you were performing a standard jump – but then kick your legs out in opposite directions, finishing at the top of your leap by doing the splits in mid-air.

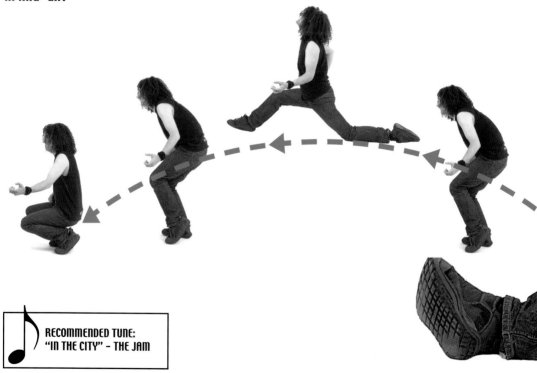

♪ RECOMMENDED TUNE:
"IN THE CITY" - THE JAM

The Duckwalk

Don't question whether or not this is cool – it just is. A vital addition to anyone's repertoire and the standard strut of choice for many guitar greats, including Chuck Berry and Angus Young.

Start off with a mincing walk, placing one foot dead in front of the other. With every beat, jut your neck forward and stick out your chin. Bring it back for the next beat, and repeat. At each step, your neck bobs forward – if you are doing this correctly, you should look a bit like a pigeon (but cooler).

RECOMMENDED TUNE:
"UP TO MY NECK IN YOU"
– AC/DC

Faces

Drop a few of these extremely sexy expressions into your playing and watch the crowd go wild!

The Kiss
Like "The Pout" but better. This is best done during a stunning solo when the TV cameras are full on you. Look directly into the lens, pucker up and blow a kiss for the adoring fans at home.

> ♪ RECOMMENDED TUNE:
> "WALK THIS WAY" –
> AEROSMITH

Looking to Heaven

Sometimes your own brilliance will cause your eyes to roll back in your head - you have no choice but to gaze up at the god of music in his rock heaven and give thanks.

Also used during particularly difficult riffs, when you can look up for inspiration. In both cases, the jaw should be slack, the gob should be open and your tongue should be lolling.

RECOMMENDED TUNE:
"DON'T FEAR THE REAPER"
- BLUE OYSTER CULT

The Tongue Waggle

Truly, deeply sexy. If you ever get to view footage of Kiss's Gene Simmons, you will see this tonguework elevated to its highest form. Stick your tongue out, and let the tip of it flicker up and down like a rattlesnake's tail. Practise this move in front of your dog - if it leaves the room in a hurry, you are probably getting it right.

RECOMMENDED TUNE:
"LICK IT UP" - KISS

Imagine you are tasting something and can't decide if it is very delicious or truly nasty.

6 Advanced

Okay, you should now be a hard-rocking, snake-hipped expert, and as such you are ready for the masterclass. The following techniques have been gathered together after exhaustive study of the world's top exponents. Few mortals ever progress to this stage, and you should exercise caution – some of the techniques that follow will be dangerous for the uninitiated. The authors and the publisher cannot accept any liability for loss or injury incurred while attempting these moves. Practise hard, my pupil. Pull these off, and you will join the pantheon of masters; get them wrong, and you will probably look like a wally.

RECOMMENDED TUNE:
"SWEET CHILD O' MINE"
– GUNS 'N' ROSES

Kneeling

Sometimes, during a great riff, you will need to fall to your knees in supplication to your instrument and your own talent. If you have been dashing about the stage in the prescribed manner, this will also give you a much-needed breather. This stance works particularly well with the "Eyes Looking up to Heaven" face.

WORD OF CAUTION! THIS CAN BE A BIT HARD ON THE KNEES – IN THE EARLY STAGES, YOU MIGHT WANT TO USE KNEEPADS OR A STRATEGICALLY PLACED PILLOW TO PROTECT YOUR KNEECAPS.

Stances

They may look like child's play, but don't be fooled – these expert stances will tax your muscles.

The Vertical Hold

This is an important variation on the standard stance. Take your guitar from its normal horizontal position and rotate it through 90 degrees - hold it out vertically, away from your left-hand side. This works superbly with the "Tongue Waggle".

NOTE! It's important to check your strap is securely fastened - if not, your air guitar may fly from your grasp.

♪ RECOMMENDED TUNE:
"BLACK BETTY"
– RAM JAM

"This can sometimes look like an involuntary convulsion"

The Classic Back Arched

When you are hanging out a long, howling, high note, your back may go into an involuntary musical spasm. Don't be alarmed - this is a perfectly natural reaction, and you will find yourself adopting the classic "Back Arched" stance. It is best used with the "Intense Sexual Ecstasy" face (see end of section).

RECOMMENDED TUNE:
"ALL RIGHT NOW" - FREE

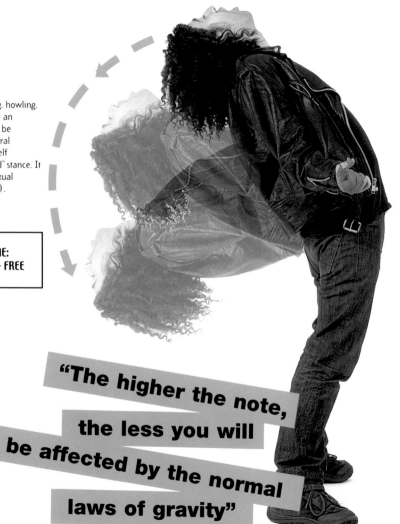

"The higher the note, the less you will be affected by the normal laws of gravity"

Sliding to Kneel

This is tricky, but looks so impressive it is worth working at. A slippery floor is the ideal surface for pulling this off – if you try this on the carpet at home you run the risk of serious knee abrasions, which may cut short your career.

Start stage left, and run across to stage right. Fall to your knees as you go, sliding the last few metres and ending up lying prone with your legs folded beneath you.

RECOMMENDED TUNE: "LOVE REMOVAL MACHINE" – THE CULT

"Make sure that you have enough runway"

"Kneeling at the altar of rock"

51

Playing behind Head

Like the title says, whip the air guitar over your head (be careful you don't get your hair caught in the strings). Perfect when coupled with "The Overbite" or "The Sneer".

"Jimi's finest contribution to the art"

When you have blown everyone away with your magic fingers, flip the guitar up so you are looking at the strings. Now pick away using your teeth rather than your right hand.

WORD OF CAUTION! THIS MOVE IS NOT SUITABLE FOR AIR GUITAR PLAYERS WHO WEAR DENTURES.

RECOMMENDED TUNE: "PURPLE HAZE" – JIMI HENDRIX EXPERIENCE

"Has the added advantage of flossing your teeth as you play"

Smashing Your Guitar

You're hot, you're sweaty, you're emotionally drained. You have thrilled an imaginary 10,000-seat stadium and there is only one way to finish – with a flourish! Take your guitar by the neck and smash the hell out of it – and out of any amplifier or air drumkit that gets in your way.

"For your big finale"

"When
off
of destru

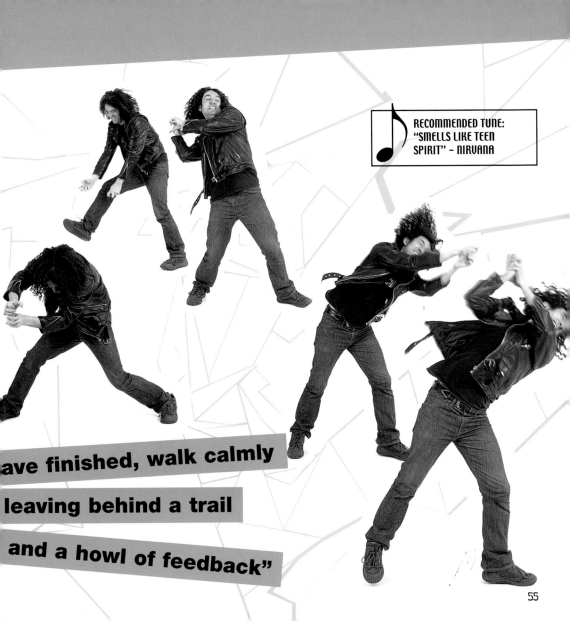

ave finished, walk calmly

leaving behind a trail

and a howl of feedback"

Faces

A great performer really feels the music – and as you are now
fast approaching rock god status, you will need some advanced
faces to match your virtuosity.

Strangling a Chicken
Sometimes you will need two hands to
tame your instrument. It's dirty work,
but someone's got to do it. Only one
particular facial expression will do.

RECOMMENDED TUNE:
"ENTER SANDMAN"
– METALLICA

"Man

become c

"For when you
need both hands"

Intense Sexual Pleasure
For a change of mood - this expression is ideal for poignant solos or ballads. Your union with your instrument is so complete it is almost embarrassing to watch (for over 18s only).

> ♪ RECOMMENDED TUNE:
> "STAIRWAY TO HEAVEN" –
> LED ZEPPELIN (SOLO ONLY)

I Can't Believe What my Hands are Playing
You are now such a maestro that your skill can astound even yourself. Look at your left hand as if it has become possessed by a greater force and is playing almost by itself.

> ♪ RECOMMENDED TUNE:
> "ERUPTION" – VAN HALEN

guitar

"Your hand may become possessed by a greater force"

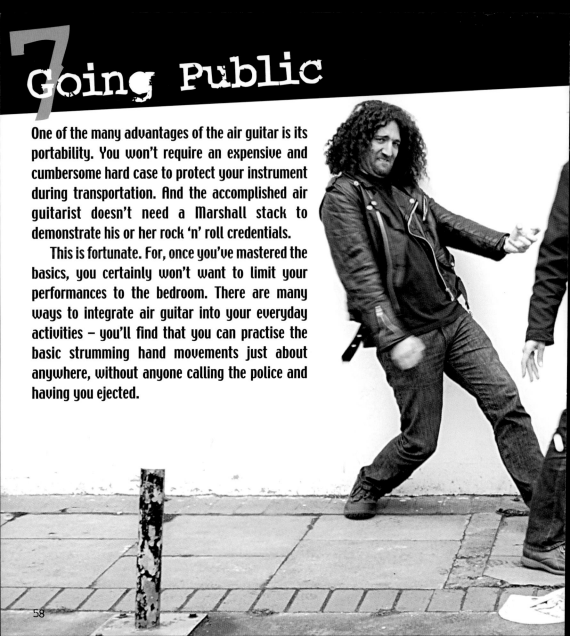

7 Going Public

One of the many advantages of the air guitar is its portability. You won't require an expensive and cumbersome hard case to protect your instrument during transportation. And the accomplished air guitarist doesn't need a Marshall stack to demonstrate his or her rock 'n' roll credentials.

This is fortunate. For, once you've mastered the basics, you certainly won't want to limit your performances to the bedroom. There are many ways to integrate air guitar into your everyday activities – you'll find that you can practise the basic strumming hand movements just about anywhere, without anyone calling the police and having you ejected.

Wembley Arena is proud to present for one night only
LIVE and UNPLUGGED
THE AMAZING • THE INVISIBLE
Matt
Russell
Experience
PLUS SUPPORT: ROBERT PLANT • CARLOS SANTANA •
PETE TOWNSEND • BRIAN MAY and many more

Around The World

The World is Your Lobster!

Air guitar is a universal language, capable of spanning the millennia and crossing the continents. You are now part of that happy, vainglorious brotherhood of performers. Now it is up to you to go forth and share your precious gift with the world. Remember – use this force only for good.

Practise, Practise, Practise!

So now you've worked through the exercises in this book. You've mastered the basics, you can breeze confidently through the more advanced moves, and you can solo along with the all-time guitar virtuosos without breaking either sweat or a string. We're confident that by now you're playing competently – entertaining yourself and those around you with air guitar performances that combine energy and technique with stunning results.

However, there's only so much we can teach you. After all, if all you needed to become a star was a book, then everybody would be on stage and there would be nobody in the audience.

How you develop as an air guitarist is up to you. But there are just a few tips we can give you to send you on your way to superstardom.

It's vital to remember that in any field, even the most accomplished practitioners are continually developing their skills and learning new techniques. Practising your moves and solos is the key to a smooth perform-ance and ensures that your playing won't stagnate.

After all, Angus Young spent years working out how to play without getting tangled up in his school tie. Likewise, Jimi Hendrix was a jobbing session musician going nowhere fast until he mastered two of the most difficult moves in this book – playing with his teeth, and behind his head. From there, it was just a short step to worldwide acclaim and as many sexual encounters as he could handle.

Do not fear the unknown!

Push yourself. Try new moves. Experiment with new facial expressions and mix existing elements of your repertoire to create something genuinely fresh.

The mark of true genius is an artist who takes all that has come before and moulds the form into something completely new, pushing boldly into uncharted territory without fear of failure or embarrassment. There is even a rumour that Marilyn Manson was grounded for two weeks when his mother saw what he'd done with her make-up and old corsets. But it didn't stop him building an act around them.

So there you have it – the complete guide to "How To Play Air Guitar". You're armed with all the tools you need to create your own rock 'n' roll legend. All that's left for you to do is to strap on that air guitar, make sure you're in tune, take the stage and show that crowd what you can really do . . . LET'S ROCK!!!

Resources

Through the miracle of modern technology, you can join hands with your brothers and sisters to learn more and to share your love of this global instrument. Check out the websites below for alternative insights into the fine and noble art of air guitar.

Send someone an air guitar by e-mail at: www.airguitar.com

Learn about the correct use of props and the international appeal of the air guitar at: www.tt92.demon.co.uk/airgtr01.htm

The air guitar has been immortalised in a line dance — learn the steps at: www.geocities.com/Nashville/5970/airguitar

Women! Find out what your man's air guitar technique tells you about his personality at: www.stim.com/menwomens/guitar/guitarstory.html

Here, for the historians among you, is a brief history of the air guitar's predecessor, the air lute: www.onr.com/user/steveh/airlute.htm

Finally, see if you can work out what this is all about: http://imagineproject.org/guitar.html